What's Really in Our Bread?

Educator & Parent Companion Guide

Teaching Materials & Resources

Supporting inquiry-based learning about food systems, agriculture, and health for ages 8-12

By David Upthegrove

Published by Upthegrove Press

ISBN 97989934904-1-0

Cross-reference: What's Really In Our Bread? ISBN 9798993490403

Worksheet downloads: www.whatsreallyinourbread.com

Teacher Quick Reference

Quick unit snapshot:

• Ages: 8-12

• Timeframe: 2-4 class sessions (45-60 min each)

• Core activities: read-aloud, produce-wash observational experiment, small research/project/poster

• Key aims: inquiry-based learning, media literacy, food-system awareness; avoid alarm, emphasize evidence-informed choices

Top 5 teacher-ready sources (brief) — see Section 5 for the full bibliography and links:

1. Lehman et al. - low-dose mouse gut microbiome (PMC)

2. Puigbo et al. - human microbiota review (PMC)

3. Walsh et al. - gut microbiome review (PMC)

4. IARC Monograph (2015) - classification overview

5. EPA Glyphosate Registration Review - regulatory details (EPA)

Suggested teacher script: "Science is a process. Some studies show possible effects; others show different results. We will look at age-appropriate evidence and focus on practical steps to reduce risk while research continues."

Table of Contents

Section 1: Quick Start Guide

Welcome, Educators!

This companion guide supports the children's book What's Really in Our Bread? by providing ready-to-use lesson plans, student activities, and background information. The materials are designed to:

✓ Spark curiosity about food systems without causing alarm

✓ Support inquiry-based, age-appropriate learning

✓ Align with common core and NGSS standards

✓ Provide balanced, science-based information

 Engage families in meaningful conversations about food

How to Use This Guide

For a 2-4 class session unit: Go straight to Section 2 (Teacher Lesson Plan) for complete, ready-to-implement lessons.

For parent engagement: Use Section 4 (Parent Communication Materials) for newsletters, parent nights, or take-home activities.

For background & deeper understanding: Read Section 3 (Background Information) to understand the science and current debates around agricultural chemicals.

Safety & Sensitivity Note

This curriculum involves NO chemical handling. All experiments are observational only. The book and lessons present agricultural chemicals (specifically glyphosate/Roundup) as a real-world example, focusing on empowerment through knowledge and practical actions rather than fear.

What You'll Need

One class set of the children's book (or single copy for read-aloud)

Student worksheets from Section 2 (print-ready)

Downloads: www.whatsreallyinourbread.com

Basic supplies for produce wash experiment (apples, water, and bowls)

Optional: wheat/barley seeds for sprouting activity

Poster materials for final project Section 2: Teacher-Facing Lesson Plan

Section 2: Teacher-Facing Lesson Plan

"Bread, Farms & Us" — Ages 8-12

Overview

This plan supports a short unit (2-4 class sessions) built around the 28-page narrative about three children exploring bread, farming, and chemicals (focused example: glyphosate). Lessons are inquiry-driven, low-risk, and designed to spark curiosity without alarm. Activities include read-aloud + guided discussion, a hands-on classroom experiment, and a small research/project that can be completed in class or as homework.

Learning Objectives

Students will explain, in their own words, where bread comes from and the main steps from field → table.

Students will identify at least two ways agricultural chemicals can enter the food system and discuss simple actions to reduce exposure.

Students will observe and record changes in a simple food-handling experiment and use evidence to draw conclusions.

Students will complete a small research poster or presentation that communicates one local or personal action to support healthier food choices.

Standards Alignment

CCSS ELA: Reading comprehension, informational text, speaking & listening (grade-appropriate standards for 3-6, e.g., RL/RI and SL strands)

NGSS: Connections to life-science concepts (ecosystems, growth, human impacts) and engineering/design practices for problem solving

(Adapt to your district's specific standards as needed.)

Materials Needed

One class set of the narrative book (or a single copy for read-aloud)

Student worksheet (see pages 12-19) — printed

Chart paper / whiteboard and markers

Materials for Produce Wash Experiment: fruit (apple or pear) per pair, bowls, tap water, optional baking-soda solution, paper towels, magnifiers

Materials for Grow-a-Grain or sprouting jars: wheat/barley seeds, jars with mesh/cheesecloth, water

Poster paper or slide template, markers, colored pencils, internet/library access (optional)

Optional: photos showing stages (seed, field, combine, mill, bakery, loaf)

Timeframe

Session 1 (45-60 min): Read-aloud + guided discussion + worksheet comprehension

Session 2 (30-45 min): Produce Wash Experiment + observation log

Session 3 (45-90 min total across class/home): Project planning and poster work; presentations (can be spread over multiple days)

Lesson Procedures

Session 1 — Read & Discuss (45-60 min)

1. Warm-up (5 min): Ask students to name everything that goes into a sandwich or slice of bread. Record responses on chart paper.

2. Read-aloud (20-25 min): Read the narrative aloud (or have students follow along). Pause at key moments (planting, farm work, chemical use, family meals) to check comprehension.

3. Guided discussion (10-15 min): Use questions from the worksheet:

• What surprised you about where bread comes from?

• Who are the people involved in getting bread to our table?

• What did the children do to learn more? How could you do the same?

4. Vocabulary check (5 min): Review glossary terms (simple definitions + pronunciations from worksheet).

5. Worksheet time (10 min): Hand out and complete the comprehension portion (Part A) in pairs or individually.

Session 2 — Produce Wash Experiment (30-45 min)

1. Safety talk (2 min): NO tasting; wash hands; use safe classroom procedures.

2. Demonstration (5 min): Show students the setup: one fruit remains unwashed, one fruit is washed under running water (or with baking-soda rinse if allowed).

3. Observation (10-15 min): Students work in pairs to conduct the experiment and record visible differences with magnifiers. Note: this experiment shows what can be seen (dirt, wax) but does NOT remove all chemical residues.

4. Class discussion (10 min): What did washing remove? What might it NOT remove? Why does variety in diet help reduce single-source exposure? Record hypotheses on chart paper.

5. Optional extension: Start Grow-a-Grain jars as a longer-term observation project (students maintain jars and log growth over 1-2 weeks).

Session 3 — Project: Local Food Choices Poster (45-90 min)

1. Explain project (10 min): Review goals and rubric (research + visuals + one action idea). Provide worksheet poster template (Part E).

2. Research time (15-20 min): Students work in small groups or pairs to research using short library/internet time or provided print sources.

3. Create poster (20-30 min): Design and create poster with visuals, key facts, and action steps.

4. Presentations (20-30 min): Each group presents (2-3 minutes) and class provides feedback.

5. Gallery walk (optional): Display posters around classroom for peer review.

Assessment & Rubrics

Formative Assessment

✓ Participation in read-aloud and guided discussion

✓ Worksheet completion (Parts A-C)

✓ Experiment observations and hypothesis formation

Summative Assessment: Research Poster/Presentation

Scored on 16-point scale (4 categories × 4 points each):

Total possible: 16 points (13-16 = A, 10-12 = B, 7-9 = C, 4-6 = D)

Differentiation Strategies

For Struggling Readers:

• Read in small groups with teacher or aide support

• Provide simplified vocabulary cards with images

• Use graphic organizers for comprehension

• Allow oral responses instead of written

For Advanced Students:

• Add data-interpretation task (e.g., chart hypothetical residue levels and discuss trends)

• Research deeper into farming practices (IPM, organic, cover cropping)

• Create additional materials (infographic, video, podcast)

• Lead a school-wide awareness campaign

For English Learners:

• Provide bilingual vocabulary list

• Pair with stronger English readers for support

• Allow responses in native language with translation support

• Use visual aids and hands-on activities extensively

Student Worksheets (Ready to Print)

The following worksheets are designed to be printed and distributed to students. They align with the three-session lesson plan and can be completed individually or in pairs.

Student Worksheet — "Bread, Farms & Us" (Ages 8-12)

Name: _____Date: _____ Class: _____

Part A — Quick Comprehension (from today's story)

1. Write 3 steps in the order that wheat becomes bread:

a. _____

b. _____

c. _____

2. Who were the three children curious about bread? Pick one and write one thing they did to learn more:

Child: _____ Action: _____

3. Circle the best answer:

a. Farmers use chemicals to: (help crops grow / make food taste sweet / clean bread)

b. Washing produce will remove: (visible dirt / all chemical residues / food nutrients)

Part B — Vocabulary Match (draw a line)

Match each word to its meaning:

1. Desiccant — (a) a person who bakes bread

2. Herbicide — (b) something that dries plants to make harvesting easier

3. Microbiome — (c) a chemical used to kill weeds

4. Residue — (d) tiny living things (like bacteria) inside you or soil

5. Glyphosate — (e) traces of something left on food or in soil

(Teacher note: Answers: 1-b, 2-c, 3-d, 4-e, 5-c; glyphosate is an herbicide)

Pronunciations (say them aloud):

• Desiccant (DEH-sih-kant)

• Herbicide (HER-bih-side)

• Microbiome (MY-kroh-bye-ome)

• Residue (REH-zih-doo)

• Glyphosate (GLY-fo-sate)

Part C — Produce Wash Experiment Log

Pair/Group: _____ Fruit type: _____

1. Describe the fruit BEFORE washing (color, spots, smell):

_____

_____

2. Washing method used (circle one): Running water / Water + gentle scrub / Baking-soda rinse

3. What did you see after washing? (visible dirt gone? shine? anything else?)

_____

_____

4. What can washing do? What can it NOT do? Write one idea for each:

Washing can: _____

Washing may NOT: _____

5. Draw or paste two small photos or sketches:

Part D — Scavenger Hunt (Take-home or in-class)

Find 3 breads or grain products at home or in the store and list the brand and what country of origin or label it shows (look at the package):

1. Brand: _____ Origin/Label: _____

2. Brand: _____ Origin/Label: _____

3. Brand: _____ Origin/Label: _____

Bring one package or a photo to class and be ready to share one thing you noticed about labels.

Part E — Mini Research Poster Planner (group work)

Topic or farm/ingredient you researched: _____

1. One sentence summary of what you learned:

_____

_____

2. One picture or drawing idea for your poster:

_____

3. One small action our class or family could do to help (pick one):

Start a small school sprouting station

Choose one organic item at the store weekly

Ask the cafeteria to list where bread ingredients come from

Other: _____

Who will do each job on your poster? (titles: researcher, artist, presenter)

Researcher: _____

Artist: _____

Presenter: _____

Part F — My Food Action Pledge (short)

I, _____, will try one thing this week to help make my food healthier:

_____

_____

(Signature) _____

Answer Key: Student Worksheets (Teacher Notes)

Overview: This consolidated Answer Key provides suggested answers, teacher notes, common misconceptions, and differentiation suggestions for Parts A-F of the student worksheets.

Part A - Quick Comprehension (Suggested answers & teacher notes):

1. Example sequence: (a) Wheat is harvested (b) Wheat is milled into flour (c) Flour is made into bread

Teacher notes: Look for students to sequence logical processing steps. If a student lists baking before milling, prompt: "What do you need to make flour?"

2. Example answer: Name one of the three children and one action they took (e.g., asked a farmer, read a label, observed a field).

Teacher notes: Accept a range of answers; use follow-up questions to probe evidence and sources.

3. Multiple choice: a) help crops grow - b) visible dirt

Teacher note: Emphasize that washing removes visible dirt and some surface residues but does not guarantee removal of systemic residues; frame as an evidence-informed, precautionary practice.

Part B - Vocabulary Match (Answers): 1-b, 2-c, 3-d, 4-e, 5-c

Teacher notes: Reinforce pronunciations and use visual cues for ELL students. For advanced students, ask them to use each term in a new sentence.

Part C - Produce Wash Experiment (Teacher notes):

Expected observations: Visible dirt, wax, or stickers may be removed; surface shine may increase. There is no simple classroom test that demonstrates removal of systemic residues. Use this activity to teach the limits of observation and experimental inference.

Common misconceptions: Students may assume "no residue = safe"; discuss dose, exposure routes, and the difference between surface and systemic residues.

Differentiation: Provide a checklist for students who need structure; offer data-interpretation extensions for advanced learners.

Part D - Scavenger Hunt (Teacher notes):

Accept varied answers. Focus feedback on observation quality: Did students note country of origin? Organic labeling? Ingredient lists?

Assessment tip: Have students share one surprising finding and explain why it matters.

Part E - Mini Research Poster Planner (Teacher notes):

Use the rubric provided in the assessment section. Look for: accurate summary, clear visuals, one evidence-informed action, and teamwork.

Extension: Ask advanced groups to include one citation from Section 5 or the website.

Part F - My Food Action Pledge (Teacher notes):

Accept small, feasible actions. Schedule a 10-minute reflection in a follow-up lesson to discuss what worked and what students learned.

Section 3: Background Information for Educators

This section provides essential background on glyphosate, the primary agricultural chemical featured in the children's book. It is designed to help educators understand the current scientific and regulatory landscape, answer parent questions, and maintain a balanced, evidence-based approach to teaching about food and agriculture.

Glyphosate: Essential Overview for Educators

This overview provides the key information you need to understand glyphosate (the active ingredient in Roundup®), the world's most widely used herbicide.

What is it?

Active ingredient in Roundup® and other herbicides; used on crops, lawns, and public spaces since the 1970s.

Where is it found?

• GM (genetically modified) crops: corn, soy, canola, cotton

• Non-GMO crops: oats, wheat, lentils, chickpeas (often used as a pre-harvest desiccant)

• Public spaces: parks, schoolyards, roadsides

• Home gardens and lawns

Common Exposure Routes:

• Food residues (especially in non-organic grains and pulses)

• Drinking water (runoff from agricultural and residential use)

• Direct contact in treated areas (playgrounds, parks, lawns)

Regulatory Status:

Approved for use by the U.S. EPA and most regulatory agencies globally. However, the World Health Organization's International Agency for Research on Cancer (IARC) classified glyphosate as 'probably carcinogenic to humans' in 2015, creating ongoing regulatory debate.

Health Concerns Raised in Research

The scientific community continues to study potential health effects of glyphosate exposure. Here's what educators should know:

Cancer Risk:

Some studies have linked glyphosate to non-Hodgkin lymphoma, particularly among agricultural workers with high occupational exposure. This has led to major lawsuits against Bayer/Monsanto with multi-billion dollar verdicts and settlements. However, regulatory agencies like the EPA have maintained that glyphosate is not likely to be carcinogenic when used according to label directions.

Endocrine Disruption:

Some laboratory and animal studies suggest glyphosate may interfere with hormone systems. The significance of these findings for human health at typical environmental exposure levels is debated.

Gut Health:

Emerging research suggests glyphosate may impact beneficial gut bacteria (microbiome). Glyphosate works by disrupting the 'shikimate pathway' found in plants and bacteria (but not in humans). Animal studies show potential microbiome changes, but direct evidence in humans at typical dietary exposure levels is limited.

Children's Vulnerability:

Children's developing bodies may be more susceptible to environmental chemicals. Some researchers suggest that childhood exposure warrants particular attention, though specific risks are still being studied.

Neurological Effects:

Some research in animal models suggests potential developmental and neurological impacts. Human studies are limited and results are mixed. The gut-brain axis connection via microbiome changes is a topic of ongoing investigation.

Understanding the Scientific Debate

Why do different scientists and agencies reach different conclusions? Here are key factors:

Mixed Evidence:

Studies show conflicting results on health effects. This can be due to differences in exposure levels, study design, populations studied, and funding sources.

Dose Matters:

Occupational exposure (farmers, applicators) differs greatly from dietary exposure (food residues). Effects seen at high doses in animal studies may not translate to low-dose, chronic human exposure.

Regulatory Divide:

Different agencies reach different conclusions based on which studies they prioritize and how they interpret conflicting data. The EPA, EFSA (European), and IARC (WHO) have reached different conclusions.

Industry Influence:

Concerns exist about potential bias in industry-funded research. Independent academic studies sometimes show different results than industry-sponsored studies. Court documents (the 'Monsanto Papers') revealed concerning internal company practices regarding research and regulatory interactions.

Long-Term Data Gaps:

Limited long-term studies exist on cumulative, low-dose exposure effects, especially for children. Many current exposure scenarios (e.g., widespread use as a desiccant on oats) are relatively recent and haven't been studied for decades.

Practical Steps to Reduce Exposure

These are evidence-based actions that educators can share with students and families:

✓ Choose organic when possible: Especially for high-residue crops like oats, wheat, lentils, and chickpeas. Organic certification prohibits glyphosate use.

✓ Wash produce thoroughly: Reduces surface residues, though glyphosate can be systemic (inside the plant). Still, washing is always a good practice for reducing overall pesticide exposure.

✓ Filter drinking water: Use reverse osmosis or activated carbon filters to reduce pesticides in tap water.

✓ Avoid treated areas: Keep children away from freshly sprayed lawns and parks. Ask your school about their pesticide policy and request notification before application.

✓ Support organic farming: Vote with your wallet and advocate for agricultural policy changes that support safer alternatives.

✓ Use alternatives at home: Try vinegar, boiling water, or manual weeding instead of chemical herbicides in home gardens.

Important Note: These steps represent a precautionary approach. They don't require accepting or rejecting any particular interpretation of the science—they simply reduce exposure while research continues.

Litigation Overview

Understanding the legal landscape around glyphosate helps educators respond to parent questions and understand why this topic generates strong opinions.

Scope and Scale

Since IARC's 2015 classification of glyphosate as 'probably carcinogenic,' tens of thousands of U.S. lawsuits have been filed against Bayer (which acquired Monsanto in 2018). At its peak, hundreds of thousands of claims existed globally.

• Bayer has paid multi-billion dollar settlements to resolve large blocks of cases

• Many cases remain active in state and federal courts

• New claims continue to be filed

Major Legal Issues

Preemption Question: A central legal issue is whether federal pesticide law (FIFRA) and EPA labeling decisions block state-law failure-to-warn claims. This question has produced circuit splits and Bayer continues to seek U.S. Supreme Court review.

Causation Debates: Plaintiffs must prove glyphosate exposure caused their cancer (typically non-Hodgkin lymphoma). Scientific experts testify on both sides with conflicting interpretations of the same studies.

Notable Verdicts

• Johnson v. Monsanto (2018): $289 million verdict (reduced to $78 million on appeal)

• Hardeman v. Monsanto (2019): $80 million verdict (reduced to $25 million)

• Pilliod v. Monsanto (2019): $2 billion verdict (reduced to $87 million)

• Barnes case (2025): Multi-billion dollar verdict in Georgia (under appeal)

Note: Many large jury awards have been reduced on appeal, but several substantial verdicts have been upheld, demonstrating that juries find the evidence of harm compelling even as regulatory agencies maintain different conclusions.

Bayer's Response Strategy

• Pursuing appeals and seeking favorable preemption rulings

• Engaging at state legislative level to limit litigation

• Reformulating consumer lawn & garden Roundup products (removing glyphosate)

• Continuing to defend glyphosate safety for agricultural use

Health Evidence by Specific Outcome

This section provides more detailed information on specific health outcomes. It's designed for educators who want deeper understanding or need to respond to specific parent concerns.

Note on Evidence Quality: Animal, mechanistic, and microbiome studies show plausible biological pathways. Human epidemiology is strongest for certain blood cancers (e.g., non-Hodgkin lymphoma) and more limited/inconclusive for many non-cancer outcomes. Co-formulants in commercial products (surfactants like POEA) often increase toxicity in experimental systems and complicate interpretation.

Gastrointestinal (GI) Disorders / Gut Effects

What the Literature Shows:

Multiple animal and mechanistic studies report gut-microbiome alterations (dysbiosis), intestinal inflammation, changes in short-chain-fatty-acid pathways, and markers of intestinal inflammation.

Some mouse studies used doses approximating regulatory Acceptable Daily Intake and still observed microbiome shifts and low-grade intestinal inflammation. Human data are limited and mostly indirect.

Mechanism: Glyphosate's activity on the shikimate pathway (present in bacteria but not in humans) can potentially alter beneficial gut microbes. This is plausible but not yet definitively proven in human populations at typical environmental exposure levels.

Key Studies:

• Lehman et al. - Low-dose glyphosate alters mouse gut microbiota (90-day study)

• Puigbò et al. - 'Does glyphosate affect the human microbiota?' (review)

• Walsh et al. - Impact on gut microbiome (open access review)

• Tang et al., 2020 - Rat study showing intestinal inflammation + microbiome shifts

Takeaway: Plausible mechanism and consistent animal signals exist. Direct, high-quality human evidence linking glyphosate residues at typical environmental levels to clinical GI disease is currently limited.

Skin / Dermal Conditions

What the Literature Shows:

Dermal exposure is a common route for applicators. Glyphosate formulations and co-formulants can cause skin irritation. In occupational contexts, dermatitis and other skin complaints have been reported.

Much clinical/epidemiologic material consists of case reports and occupational exposure literature rather than large cohort studies. Microbiome studies show skin-associated microbes can be sensitive to glyphosate in vitro, suggesting potential for microbiome disruption.

Takeaway: Dermal irritation and occupational skin complaints are plausible and reported. Chronic dermatologic disease causation by typical environmental exposures is not well established in high-quality population studies. Other Health Endpoints (Brief Summary)

Cancer: Litigation centers on alleged links to non-Hodgkin lymphoma. IARC classified glyphosate as 'probably carcinogenic' in 2015. Regulatory bodies (EPA, EFSA) have reached different conclusions. Litigation and new studies continue.

Reproductive, Metabolic, Immunologic Effects: Animal and mechanistic studies exist showing potential effects. Human evidence is variable and often limited. These remain active areas of research.

Suggested Language for Classroom Discussions

When discussing glyphosate with students or parents, consider this balanced framing:

"Scientific and legal debates about glyphosate are ongoing. Animal and mechanistic research shows plausible pathways by which glyphosate or glyphosate-based formulations—especially with co-formulants—could alter the gut micro biome, provoke low-grade inflammation, and in some models affect nervous-system endpoints. High-quality human epidemiology for many non-cancer outcomes (GI disorders, chronic neurologic disease, chronic skin disease) is limited and findings are mixed. Evidence linking glyphosate to certain blood cancers (e.g., non-Hodgkin lymphoma) has been central to major lawsuits. The precautionary principle suggests taking reasonable steps to reduce exposure while research continues. Readers interested in the primary science and court developments should consult the sources provided in this guide."

Section 4: Parent Communication Materials

This section provides ready-to-use materials for communicating with parents about the 'What's Really in Our Bread?' unit. These materials help build understanding and support while addressing common concerns.

Sample Parent Letter

Copy and customize this letter to send home before beginning the unit

Dear Families,

Our class will soon begin an exciting inquiry-based unit called 'Bread, Farms & Us,' based on the children's book What's Really in Our Bread? This short unit (2-4 class sessions) explores where our food comes from and the journey from farm to table.

What We'll Learn:

• The steps wheat takes from field to bread

• How modern farming works and the role of agricultural chemicals

• Ways we can make informed food choices

• How to think critically about the food system

Activities Include:

• Reading and discussing the story together

• A simple produce-washing experiment (observational only—no tasting!)

• Creating a research poster about local food choices

• Optional: growing wheat or barley sprouts in the classroom

Important Notes:

✓ This is an inquiry-based unit designed to spark curiosity, not create alarm

✓ No chemicals will be used or handled in any activities

✓ We present balanced, age-appropriate, science-based information

✓ Students will learn practical actions they and their families can take

We believe this unit will help students develop critical thinking skills and a deeper appreciation for the complex systems that bring food to our tables. If you have questions or would like more information, please feel free to contact me.

At-Home Extension (Optional):

Your child will bring home a 'Scavenger Hunt' worksheet asking them to examine 3 grain products at home and notice labels, origins, and certifications. This is a fun way to extend learning beyond the classroom!

Sincerely,

[Your Name]

[Grade/Subject]

FAQ for Parents

Use these answers to respond to common parent questions and concerns:

Q: Why are you teaching young children about pesticides? Isn't this scary?

A: We're teaching about the food system in an age-appropriate, empowering way. The focus is on curiosity, critical thinking, and practical actions—not fear. Students learn that people are working to understand and improve our food system, and that small choices can make a difference. The activities are hands-on, engaging, and designed to spark wonder rather than worry.

Q: Are you telling children not to eat certain foods?

A: No. We emphasize that all foods can be part of a healthy diet. The unit teaches students to think about where food comes from and to understand labels and choices. We discuss practical steps like washing produce, choosing variety, and understanding organic vs. conventional—but never say certain foods are 'bad' or should be avoided entirely.

Q: Is this curriculum biased against farmers or agriculture?

A: Absolutely not. The book and lessons honor the hard work of farmers and present modern agriculture in context. We discuss how farmers make difficult decisions, face economic pressures, and are working to improve practices. Students learn that there are no simple answers and that many stakeholders are trying to balance productivity, economics, and environmental/health concerns.

Q: Will there be any chemicals in the classroom?

A: No. All activities are observational only. The produce-washing experiment uses only water, fruit, and optional baking soda (a common household item). We do not handle, display, or use any herbicides, pesticides, or other agricultural chemicals.

Q: What if my child asks questions I can't answer?

A: That's wonderful! Curiosity is the goal. You can explore together by reading food labels, visiting a farmers market, or looking up information together. The companion guide includes resources for families. It's okay to say 'I don't know—let's find out together.'

Q: Our family can't afford organic food. Will my child feel bad?

A: The unit emphasizes that many actions don't cost anything (washing produce thoroughly, choosing variety, asking questions) and that organic is just one option among many. We discuss economic realities and never shame or judge food choices. Students learn that everyone can take small, meaningful steps regardless of budget.

Q: What's the scientific basis for this unit?

A: The companion guide includes extensive background information with citations to peer-reviewed research, regulatory documents, and current scientific debates. We present multiple perspectives and acknowledge where evidence is strong, emerging, or uncertain. Parents are welcome to review these materials at any time.

At-Home Extension Activities

Share these activities with families who want to extend learning at home:

Grow Your Own Sprouts

Materials: Mason jar, cheesecloth or mesh, wheat or mung bean seeds, water

Instructions:

1. Rinse seeds and place in jar with water. Soak overnight.

2. Drain water, cover jar with cheesecloth secured with rubber band.

3. Rinse and drain twice daily for 3-5 days.

4. Watch seeds sprout! Discuss how plants grow and what they need.

5. Optional: Eat the sprouts in a salad (adult supervision required).

Label Detective

Activity: Go on a 'label hunt' at the grocery store or in your pantry.

Look for:

• Country of origin

• Organic certification seals

• 'Non-GMO Project Verified' labels

• Ingredient lists (how many ingredients can you recognize?)

• Nutrition facts

Discussion questions:

• What surprised you?

• Which products had the shortest ingredient lists?

• Did you find foods from other countries? How did they get here?

Bake Bread Together

Activity: Make simple bread from scratch to understand the transformation from wheat to food.

Simple No-Knead Bread Recipe:

• 3 cups flour

• 1/4 teaspoon instant yeast

• 1 1/2 teaspoons salt

• 1 1/2 cups water

Mix ingredients, cover, let rise 12-18 hours. Shape, let rise 2 hours. Bake at 450°F for 30 minutes.

While baking, discuss:

• What is the flour made from?

• Where did those ingredients come from?

• How is homemade bread different from store-bought?

Map Your Food

Activity: Track where your food comes from for one week.

• Keep a food journal

• Note country/state of origin when possible

• Mark locations on a map

• Calculate approximate distances food traveled

• Discuss: What did you learn? Were you surprised by anything?

Visit a Farmers Market or Farm

Activity: Connect with local food producers.

Questions to ask farmers:

• What do you grow?

• How do you deal with weeds and pests?

• What's the hardest part of farming?

• How long have you been farming?

Many farmers love talking to curious kids! This helps students see farming as real work done by real people.

Section 5: Additional Resources

This section provides comprehensive resources for educators who want to dive deeper, conduct additional research, or connect with community organizations.

Further Reading & Citations

These peer-reviewed studies, regulatory documents, and journalistic sources provide the scientific foundation for the information in this guide.

Litigation Resources

Bayer official litigation page:

https://www.bayer.com/en/managing-the-roundup-litigation

Reuters coverage (Supreme Court/appeals):

https://www.reuters.com/sustainability/boards-policy-regulation/bayer-renews-bid-us-supreme-court-curb-glyphosate-cases-2025-04-04/

Investigate Midwest reporting:

https://investigatemidwest.org/2025/05/07/bayers-full-court-press-to-end-glyphosate-lawsuits-heats-up/

Gut / Microbiome Evidence

Lehman et al. (low-dose mouse study):

https://pmc.ncbi.nlm.nih.gov/articles/PMC10330715/

Puigbò et al. (human microbiota review):

https://pmc.ncbi.nlm.nih.gov/articles/PMC9145961/

Walsh et al. (gut microbiome review):

https://pmc.ncbi.nlm.nih.gov/articles/PMC10561581/

Tang et al. (rat intestinal inflammation):

https://pubmed.ncbi.nlm.nih.gov/32045792/

Neurological Outcomes

Chang et al. (systematic review of epidemiology):

https://www.ncbi.nlm.nih.gov/pmc/articles/PMC9823069/

Nature Reviews Neurology (call for research):

https://www.nature.com/articles/s41582-023-00919-7

Lancet Planetary Health (regulatory gaps):

https://www.thelancet.com/journals/lanplh/article/PIIS2542-5196(23)00255-3/fulltext

Regulatory Documents

EPA Glyphosate Registration Review:

https://www.epa.gov/ingredients-used-pesticide-products/glyphosate

IARC Monograph (2015 carcinogen classification):

https://www.iarc.who.int/featured-news/media-centre-iarc-news-glyphosate/

European Food Safety Authority (EFSA) assessment:

https://www.efsa.europa.eu/en/topics/topic/glyphosate

Books & Reports for Educators

• The Monsanto Papers (investigative journalism compilation)

• Whitewash: The Story of a Weed Killer, Cancer, and the Corruption of Science by Carey Gillam

• Silent Spring by Rachel Carson (historical context for pesticide awareness)

• The Omnivore's Dilemma (Young Readers Edition) by Michael Pollan

Community Connections

Building connections with local organizations enriches student learning and creates lasting impact beyond the classroom.

 Connecting with Local Farms

How to find farms:

• Search 'farms near me' or 'agritourism [your county]'

• Contact your local Extension office

• Check LocalHarvest.org for farms and farmers markets

• Ask at farmers markets about farm tours

Before visiting, ask about:

• Age-appropriate activities and safety protocols

• Pesticide use and timing (avoid recent application areas)

• Educational programs they offer

• Any costs or requirements

School Garden Programs

Starting or enhancing a school garden connects students directly to food production.

Resources:
• FoodCorps (foodcorps.org) - Connects schools with service members

• KidsGardening.org - Grants, lesson plans, and curriculum

• Life Lab (lifelab.org) - Garden-based science curriculum

• Local Master Gardener programs (often volunteer at schools)

Cooperative Extension Offices

Every U.S. county has a Cooperative Extension office (land-grant university system) that provides free agricultural and food education.

They can provide:

• Guest speakers on farming, food systems, or nutrition

• Curriculum materials and lesson plans

• 4-H program connections

• Science-based information on pesticides and agriculture

Search 'Cooperative Extension [your county]' to find your local office.

 Food Banks and Pantries

Partner with local food assistance organizations to teach about food access and equity.

Potential activities:

• Organize a food drive

• Volunteer as a class (age-appropriate roles)

• Learn about food insecurity in your community

• Donate produce from school garden

Extension Projects

These longer-term projects can extend learning across weeks or months and engage the broader school community.

Project 1: Classroom Wheat Field

Duration: 8-12 weeks

Description:

Grow wheat from seed to harvest in large containers or a raised bed. Document growth stages with photos and measurements. When mature, harvest, thresh, and winnow the grain (if possible). Calculate yield and compare to commercial farming.

Learning outcomes:

• Firsthand experience with crop lifecycle

• Understanding of agricultural challenges (pests, weather, disease)

• Math applications (growth rates, yield calculations)

• Patience and long-term observation skills

Project 2: School Food Audit

Duration: 4-6 weeks

Description:

Conduct an audit of food in the school cafeteria. Survey origins, organic options, whole foods vs. processed, and student preferences. Present findings to administration with recommendations.

Learning outcomes:

• Data collection and analysis

• Interviewing and surveying skills

• Presentation and advocacy

• Understanding institutional food systems

Project 3: Farm-to-Table Documentary

Duration: 6-8 weeks

Description:

Create a short video documentary (5-10 minutes) following one local food item from farm to table. Interview farmers, processors, distributors, and consumers. Edit and present to school or community.

Learning outcomes:

• Research and interviewing

• Video production and editing

• Storytelling and narrative structure

• Community engagement

Project 4: School Pesticide Policy Campaign

Duration: Ongoing

Description:

Research your school district's current pesticide policies for grounds maintenance. Create an awareness campaign and, if appropriate, advocate for integrated pest management (IPM) or organic approaches. Work with administration to implement changes.

Learning outcomes:

• Policy research and analysis

• Civic engagement and advocacy

• Collaboration with decision-makers

• Real-world problem solving

Note: This project requires careful framing to avoid being perceived as attacking school staff. Frame it as student-led research and partnership rather than criticism.

Conclusion

Thank you for using this companion guide! The 'What's Really in Our Bread?' unit represents an opportunity to engage students in meaningful, real-world learning about food systems, health, and environmental stewardship.

By approaching this topic with curiosity, balance, and age-appropriate framing, you're empowering students to think critically, ask questions, and take informed action. The skills they develop—research, analysis, communication, and advocacy—will serve them far beyond this unit.

Remember:

✓ This is about inquiry and empowerment, not fear

✓ Multiple perspectives exist and that's okay

✓ Small actions can make a real difference

✓ Questions are more valuable than certainty

We hope this guide supports your teaching and helps create curious, informed citizens who care about their food, their health, and their planet.

Happy Teaching!

Important Disclaimer

This companion guide is provided for educational purposes only and does not constitute legal, medical, or professional advice. The information presented reflects current scientific understanding and ongoing debates as of October 2025.

Scientific understanding of agricultural chemicals and their health effects continues to evolve. Educators should consult current sources and be prepared to update information as new research emerges.

Individual families should consult healthcare providers and make food choices based on their own values, needs, and circumstances. This guide does not prescribe specific food choices or medical advice.

Citations and links were current at time of publication. Some links may change over time. Use search engines to locate moved resources if needed.